I Used to Play Piano

40s and 50s HITS

Arranged by Carol Matz

Foreword

The *I Used to Play Piano* series was designed for adults who have studied piano before and want to play again. The *I Used to Play Piano Refresher Course Book* (#22166) includes classical pieces, jazz and ragtime, etudes, pieces by well-known contemporary composers, traditional familiar favorites, as well as instructional text about playing piano.

Now adults will have a blast playing pop favorites in the correlating book, *I Used to Play Piano: 40s and 50s Hits*. Like the *Refresher Course Book,* this hits book is organized into units, progressing gradually from elementary through late intermediate in difficulty. Familiar pieces from recordings, Broadway, movies and television are included to study simultaneously with each corresponding unit in the *Refresher Course Book.*

Through this series, adults will be inspired to rediscover the joy of playing piano with the pop music they love.

ISBN-10: 0-7390-5587-9
ISBN-13: 978-0-7390-5587-8

Alfred

Table of Contents

page

Foreword 1

Unit One
Great Balls of Fire 3

Unit Two
Blue Moon 4

Unit Three
(We're Gonna) Rock Around the Clock 6

Unit Four
I Could Have Danced All Night 8

Unit Five
My Funny Valentine 10

Unit Six
That's Entertainment 12

Unit Seven
Cruella De Vil 15

Unit Eight
Music! Music! Music! (Put Another Nickel In) 18
Laura 20

Unit Nine
Satin Doll 23

Unit Ten
Cry Me a River 26

Unit Eleven
Misty 30

Unit One

Colorful rock 'n' roll singer and pianist Jerry Lee Lewis recorded this big hit in 1957 in Memphis, Tennessee. It reached #1 and #2 on the country and pop charts respectively. Lewis, famous for his flamboyant performances (including playing the piano with his feet) was inducted into the Rock and Roll Hall of Fame in 1986.

GREAT BALLS OF FIRE

Words and Music by
Otis Blackwell and Jack Hammer
Arranged by Carol Matz

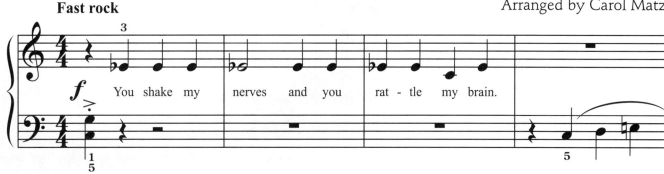

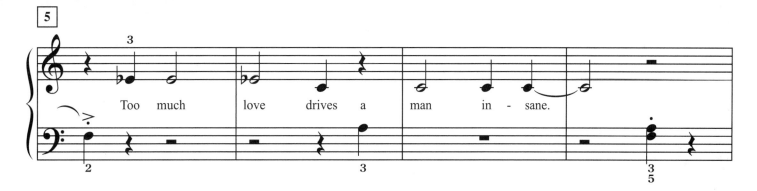

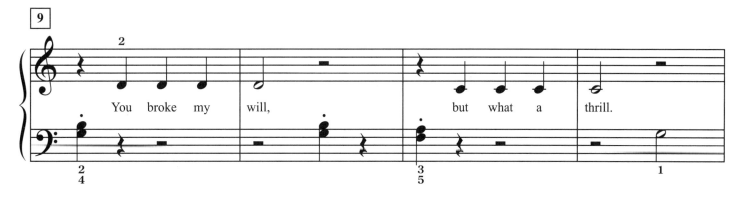

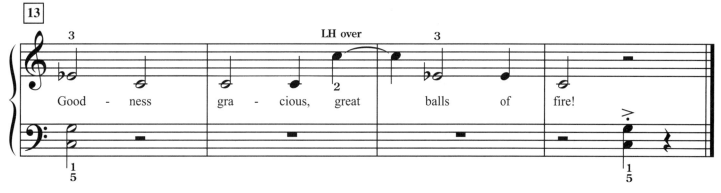

Unit Two

"Blue Moon" became a standard ballad and was recorded by numerous artists including Billie Holiday, Dizzy Gillespie, Ella Fitzgerald and Frank Sinatra. The first rock 'n' roll version of the song was recorded by Elvis Presley, but the best-remembered version is by the doo-wop group The Marcels. That record sold a million copies and is featured in the Rock and Roll Hall of Fame's "500 Songs that Shaped Rock 'n' Roll."

BLUE MOON

Music by Richard Rodgers
Lyrics by Lorenz Hart
Arranged by Carol Matz

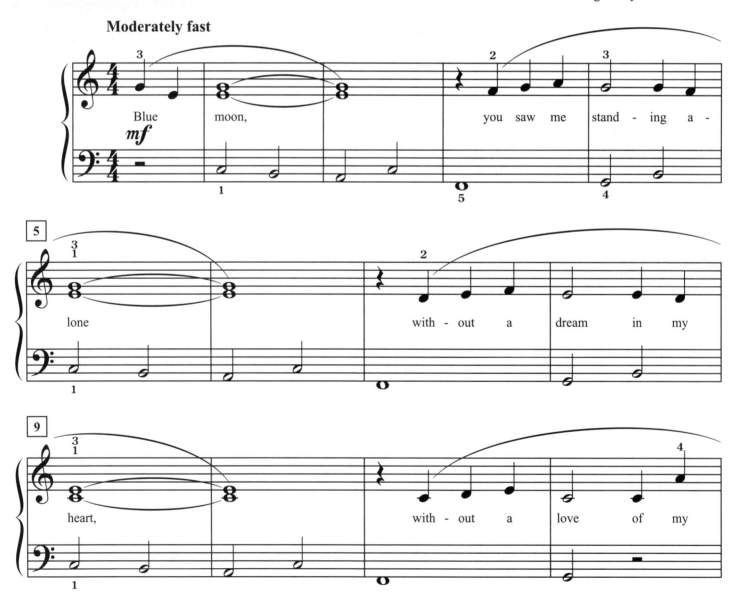

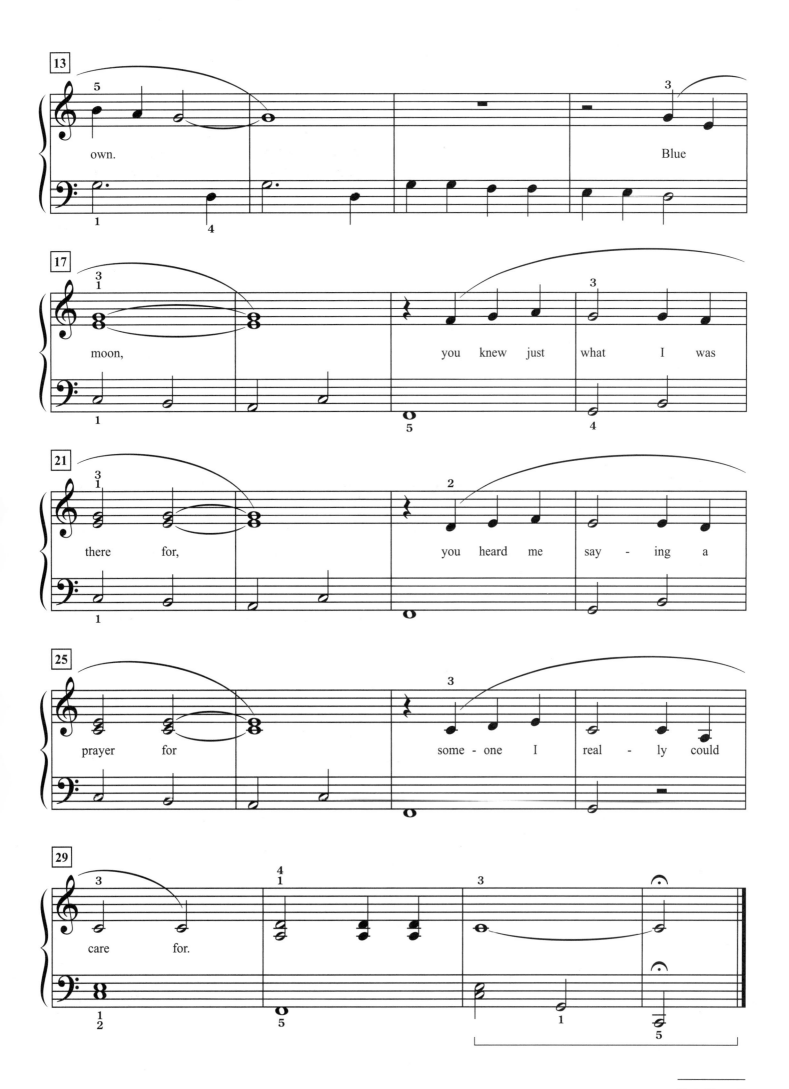

Unit Three

Considered to be one of the first rock 'n' roll songs, this hit was recorded by Bill Haley & His Comets in 1954. It spent eight weeks at the top of the Billboard charts, and has since become an all-time 50s favorite.

(We're Gonna)
Rock Around the Clock

Words and Music by
Max C. Freedman and Jimmy De Knight
Arranged by Carol Matz

* Play all eighth notes with an uneven, long-short pattern:

long-short

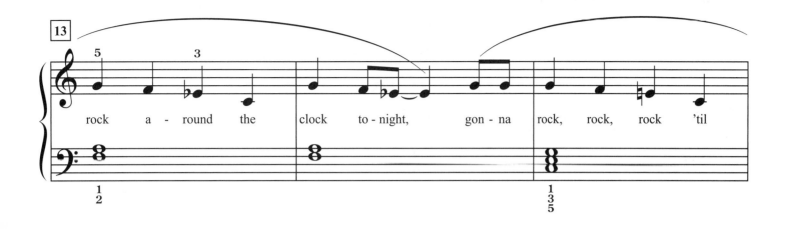

rock a - round the clock to-night, gon - na rock, rock, rock 'til

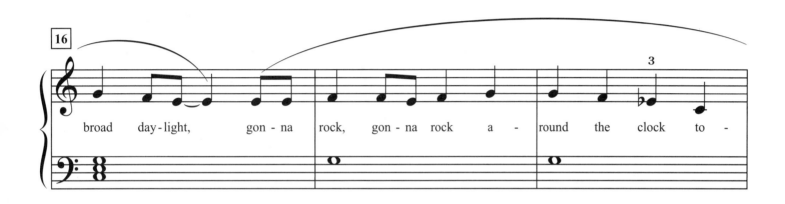

broad day-light, gon - na rock, gon - na rock a - round the clock to -

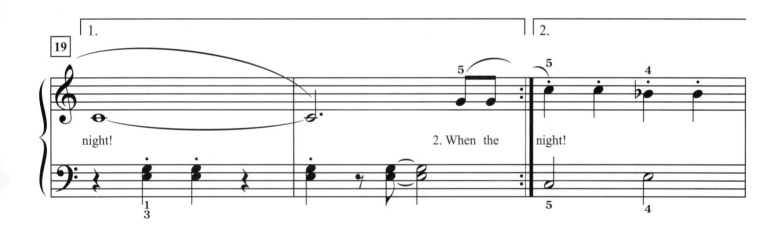

night!

2. When the night!

Unit Four

Julie Andrews first performed this classic Broadway piece in the original production of *My Fair Lady* in 1956. The piece is sung by the character Eliza Doolittle as she recalls dancing with her tutor, Henry Higgins. The 1964 film version features Audrey Hepburn as Doolittle; however, Marni Nixon actually recorded the song, which was then dubbed into the film.

I COULD HAVE DANCED ALL NIGHT

Lyrics by Alan Jay Lerner
Music by Frederick Loewe
Arranged by Carol Matz

Unit Five

The legendary songwriting team of Rodgers and Hart had already penned numerous unforgettable songs when they wrote this classic piece for the show *Babes in Arms*. The show later turned into a Hollywood film starring Judy Garland and Mickey Rooney.

MY FUNNY VALENTINE

Words by Lorenz Hart
Music by Richard Rodgers
Arranged by Carol Matz

Unit Six

This piece was written for *The Band Wagon,* a 1953 musical film starring Fred Astaire and Cyd Charisse. Over the years, "That's Entertainment" has become the one of the entertainment industry's signature pieces.

THAT'S ENTERTAINMENT

Words by Howard Dietz
Music by Arthur Schwartz
Arranged by Carol Matz

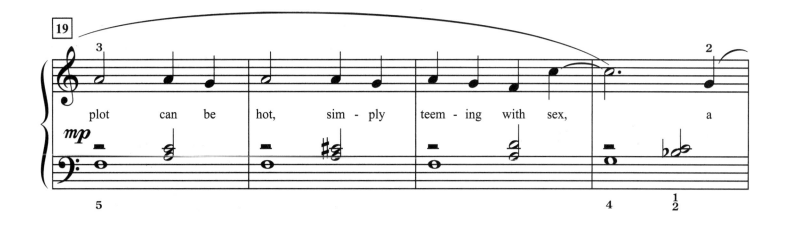

plot can be hot, sim - ply teem - ing with sex, a

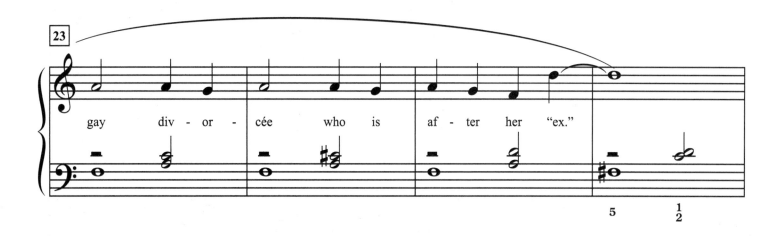

gay div - or - cée who is af - ter her "ex."

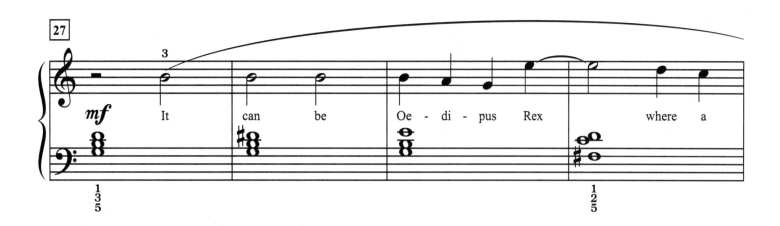

It can be Oe - di - pus Rex where a

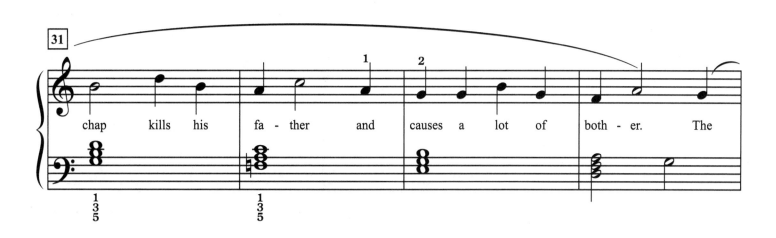

chap kills his fa - ther and causes a lot of both - er. The

A play on the words "cruel" and "devil," Cruella De Vil is the main villain in Walt Disney's animated film *One Hundred and One Dalmatians.* In 1996, Disney created a live-action film version starring award-winning actress Glenn Close as the evil Cruella.

CRUELLA DE VIL
(from Walt Disney's "101 Dalmatians")

Words and Music by Mel Leven
Arranged by Carol Matz

in - no - cent chil - dren had bet - ter be - ware. She's like a spi - der wait - ing for the

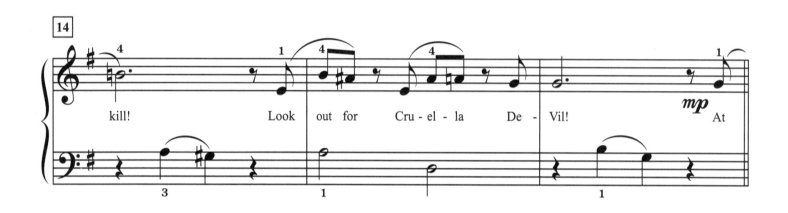

kill! Look out for Cru - el - la De - Vil! At

first you think Cru - el - la is the de - vil, but af - ter time has worn a - way the

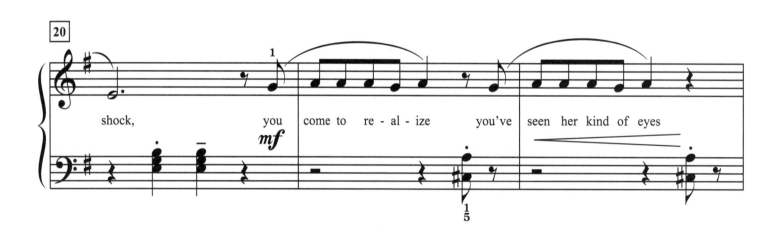

shock, you come to re - al - ize you've seen her kind of eyes

watch - ing you from un - der - neath a rock! This

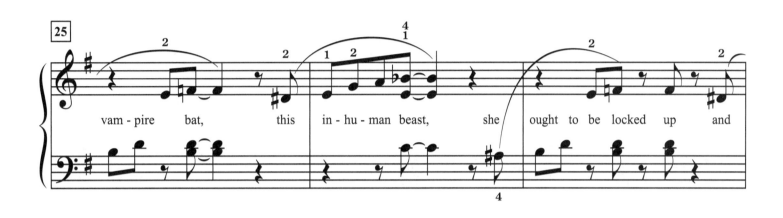

vam - pire bat, this in - hu - man beast, she ought to be locked up and

nev - er re - leased! The world was such a whole - some place un -

til Cru - el - la, Cru - el - la De - Vil!

Unit Eight

Originally recorded by Teresa Brewer in 1949, this song became a #1 hit and sold a million copies in 1950. Petula Clark recorded another version that was popular in Australia, and an instrumental version was later recorded by Bill Haley & His Comets.

MUSIC! MUSIC! MUSIC!

(Put Another Nickel In)

Words and Music by
Bernie Baum and Stephan Weiss
Arranged by Carol Matz

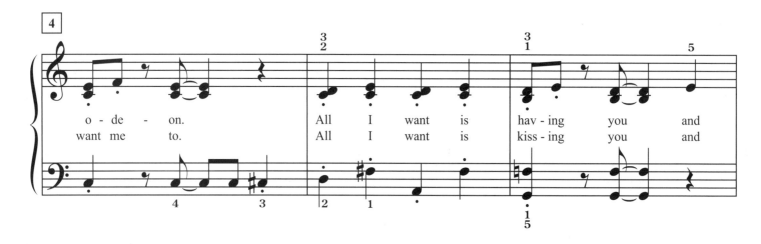

This beautiful song was adapted from the theme of the Academy Award-winning film *Laura* (1944), starring Gene Tierney and Dana Andrews. It has become a standard in the jazz repertoire and has been recorded by numerous artists including Woody Herman, Julie London, Ella Fitzgerald, Charlie Parker, Frank Sinatra, Bill Evans and others.

Laura

Lyrics by Johnny Mercer
Music by David Raksin
Arranged by Carol Matz

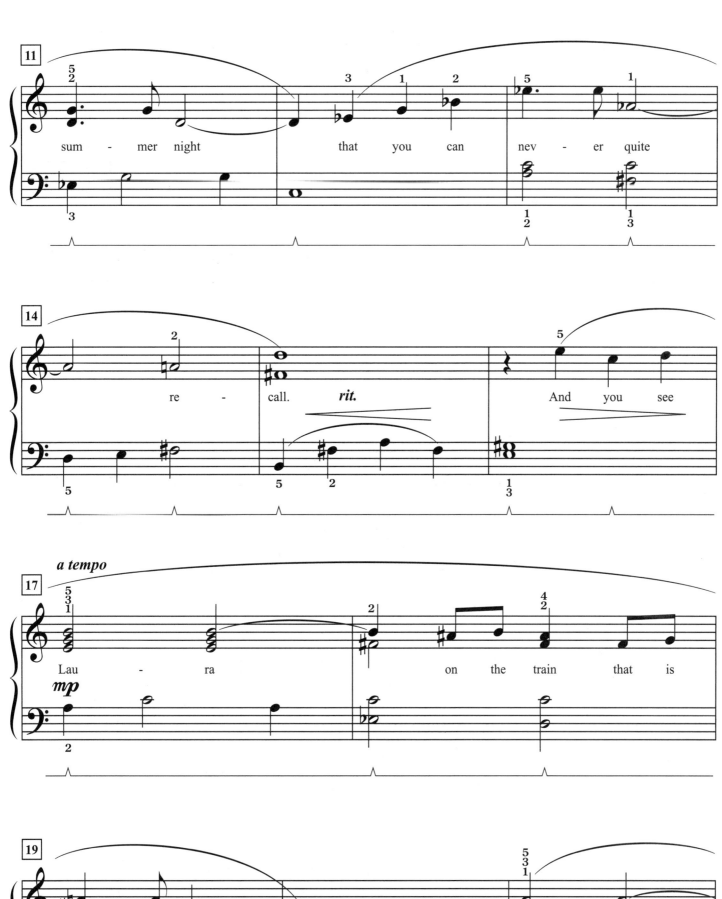

sum - mer night   that you can   nev - er quite

re - call.   *rit.*   And you see

a tempo

Lau - ra   on the train that is

pass - ing through;   those eyes,

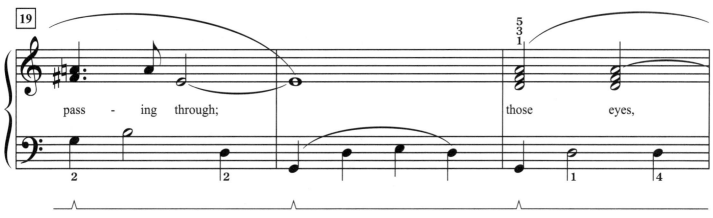

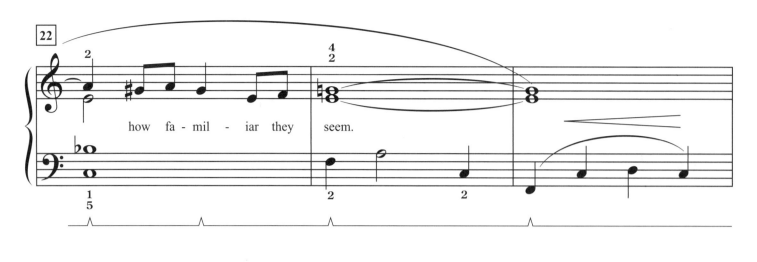

how fa - mil - iar they seem.

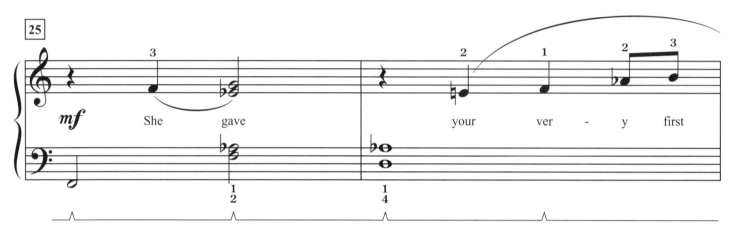

mf

She gave your ver - y first

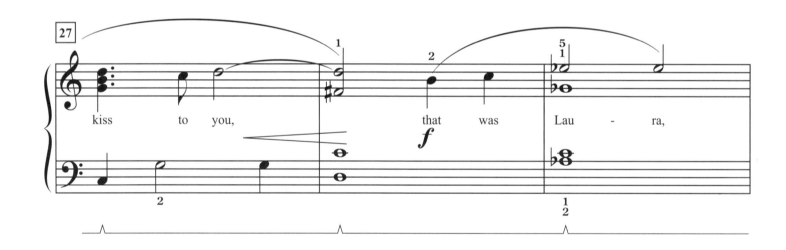

kiss to you, that was Lau - ra,

f

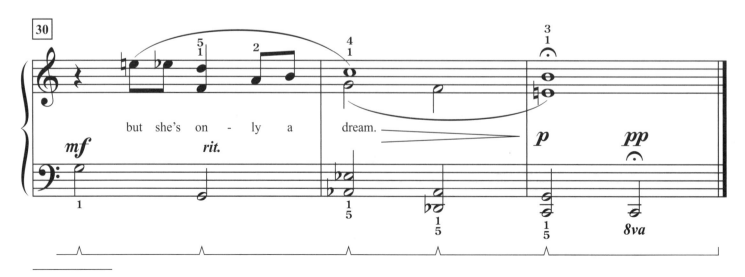

but she's on - ly a dream.

mf *rit.* *p* *pp*

8va

Unit Nine

Numerous legendary singers—including Frank Sinatra, Ella Fitzgerald and Nancy Wilson—have recorded this great jazz standard, written in 1953. A countless number of other artists have recorded instrumental versions. Renowned composer and bandleader Duke Ellington (one of the song's writers) used "Satin Doll" as the closing number at most of his performances.

SATIN DOLL

Words and Music by Johnny Mercer,
Duke Ellington and Billy Strayhorn
Arranged by Carol Matz

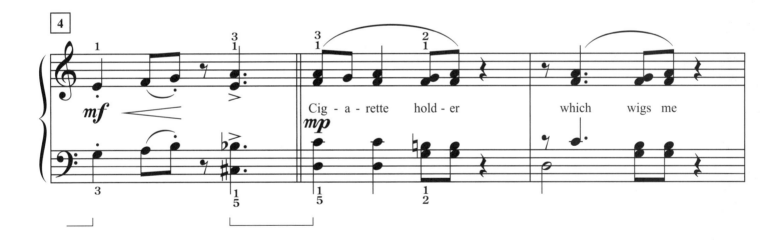

Unit Ten

The torchy blues tune "Cry Me a River" was first recorded by singer/actress Julie London in 1955. This recording was featured in the film *The Girl Can't Help It* (1956) and was released as a single the following year. . The song soon became a standard and has been recorded by many notable artists including Ella Fitzgerald, Dinah Washington, Barbra Streisand and Joe Cocker.

CRY ME A RIVER

Words and Music by Arthur Hamilton
Arranged by Carol Matz

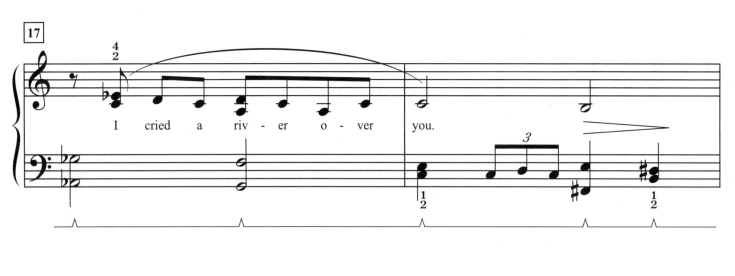

I cried a riv - er o - ver you.

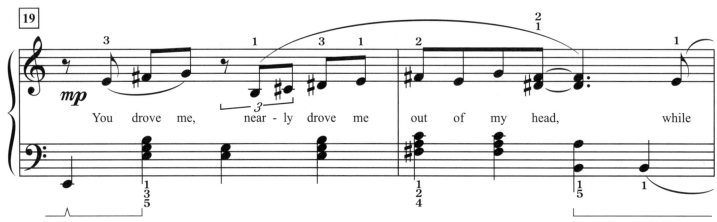

You drove me, near - ly drove me out of my head, while

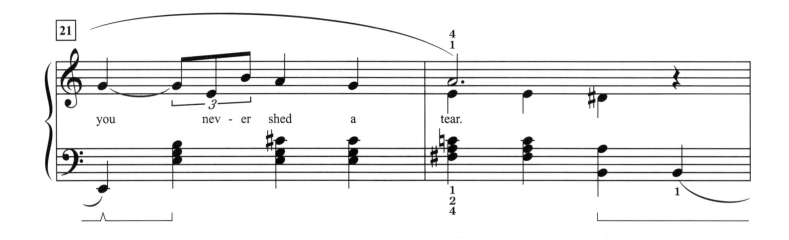

you nev - er shed a tear.

Re - mem - ber? I re - mem - ber all that you said;

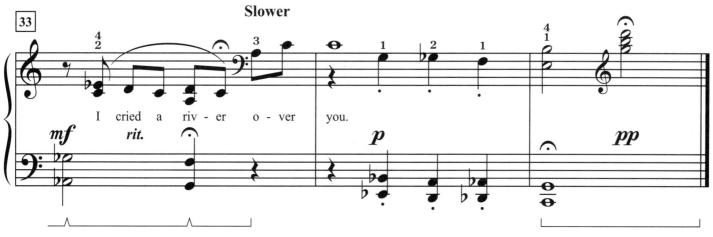

Unit Eleven

Originally composed as an instrumental piece by pianist Erroll Garner in 1954, "Misty" became a jazz vocal standard after Johnny Burke added his enduring lyrics.

MISTY

Words by Johnny Burke
Music by Erroll Garner
Arranged by Carol Matz

play.　　Or it might be the sound of your hel - lo, that

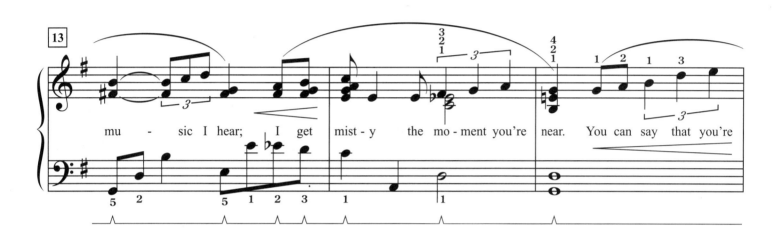

mu - sic I hear;　I get mist - y　the mo - ment you're near.　You can say that you're

lead - ing me on,　　but it's just what I　want you to do.

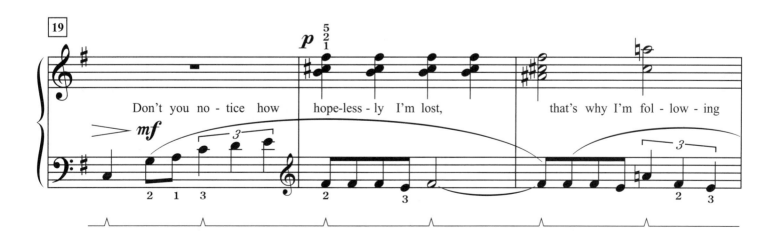

Don't you no - tice how　hope-less - ly I'm lost,　　that's why I'm fol - low - ing

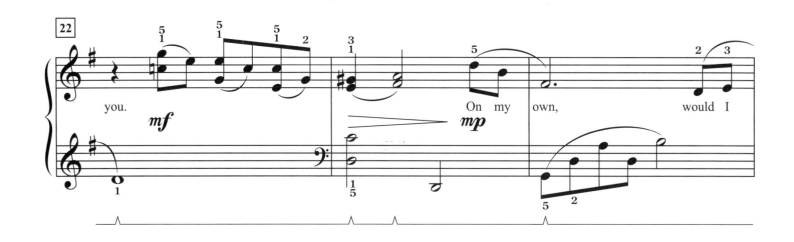

you.   *mf*   On my own,   would I

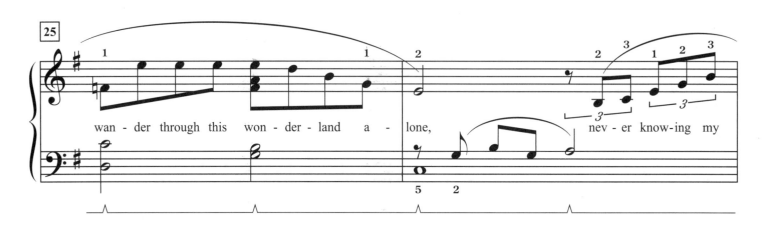

wan - der through this won - der - land a - lone,   nev - er know-ing my

right foot from my left,   my hat   from my glove, I'm too   mist - y   and too much in
rit.

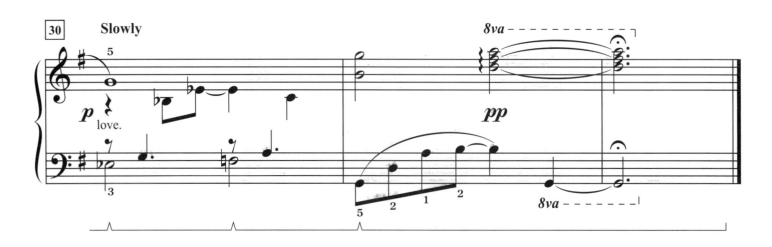

Slowly

p love.   *pp*